Dolphins

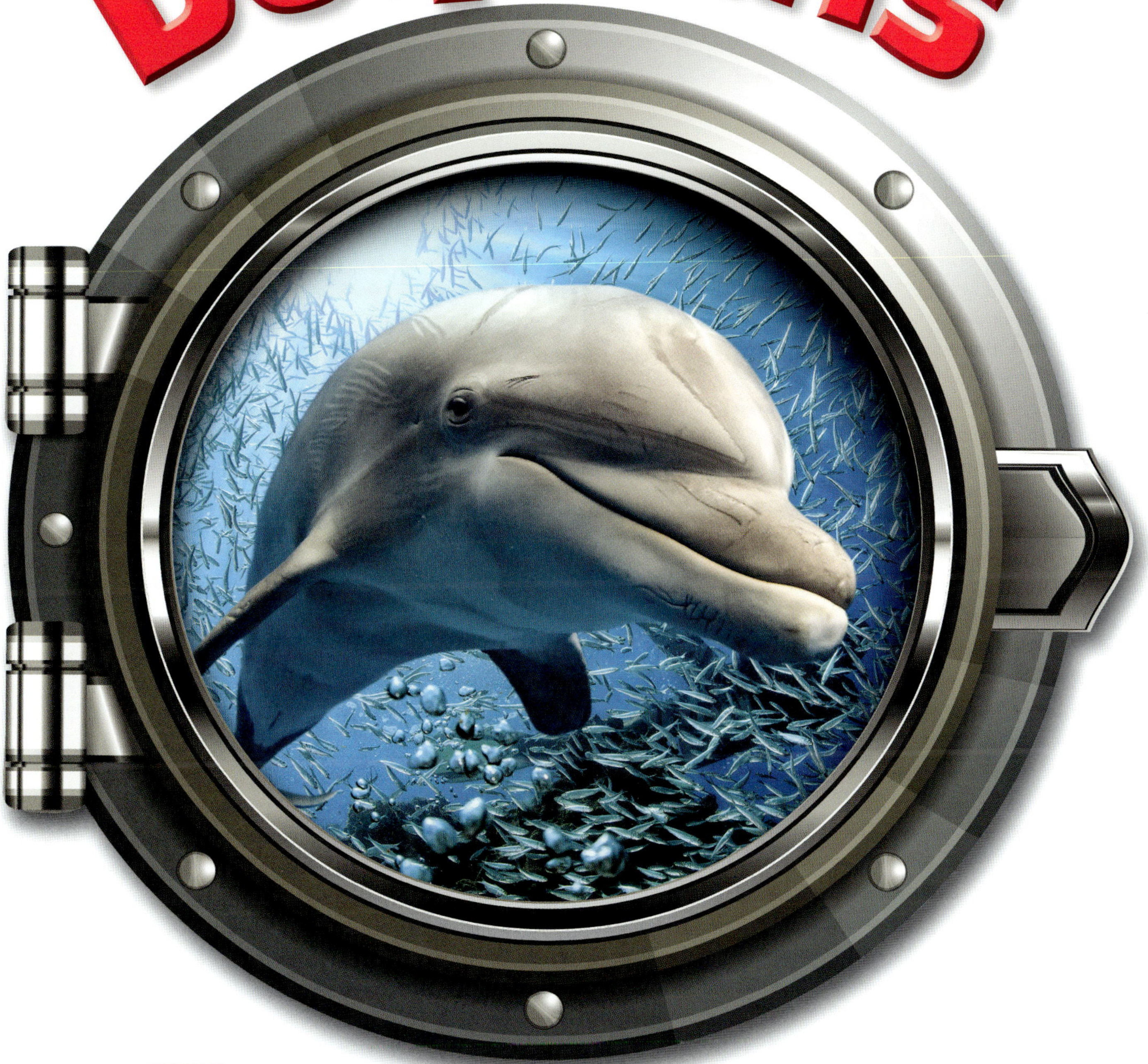

BY KARA L. LAUGHLIN

The Child's World®
childsworld.com

Published by The Child's World®
1980 Lookout Drive • Mankato, MN 56003-1705
800-599-READ • www.childsworld.com

DESIGN ELEMENTS
© creatOR76/Shutterstock.com: porthole
© keren-seg/Shutterstock.com: water

PHOTO CREDITS
© Andrea Izzotti/Shutterstock.com: cover, 1; ChameleonsEye/Shutterstock.com: 18-19; Joost van Uffelen/Shutterstock.com: 8-9, 11, 14-15; Sokolov Alexey/Shutterstock.com: 6-7; Tory Kallman/Shutterstock.com: 5, 20-21; vkilikov/Shutterstock.com: 13; Yann hubert/Shutterstock.com: 17

ISBN: 9781503816855
LCCN: 2016945859

Printed in the United States of America
PA02326

NOTE FOR PARENTS AND TEACHERS

The Child's World® helps early readers develop their informational-reading skills by providing easy-to-read books that fascinate them and hold their interest. Encourage new readers by following these simple ideas:

BEFORE READING

- Page briefly through the book. Discuss the photos. What does the reader think he or she will learn in this book? Let the child ask questions.
- Look at the glossary together. Discuss the words.

READ THE BOOK

- Now read the book together, or let the child read the book independently.

AFTER READING

- Urge the child to think more. Ask questions such as, "What things are different among the animals shown in this book?"

Contents

Wave Jumpers

A smooth gray animal moves fast in the sea. A fin on the animal's back splits the waves. The animal jumps out of the water! What is this ocean animal? It is a dolphin.

Did you know?

There are more than 30 species of dolphins.

Breathing Mammals

Dolphins look like fish. They are not. Dolphins are **mammals**. All mammals need air. Dolphins breathe through **blowholes** on top of their heads.

Did you know?

A dolphin can blow bubbles with its blowhole.

Flukes and Flippers

A dolphin swims by pumping its tail up and down. The tail has two **flukes** at the end.

Did you know?

Dolphins can swim up to 20 miles (32 kilometers) per hour.

A dolphin uses its two **flippers** to steer in the water. Dolphins are fast!

Seeing with Sound

The ocean can be dark. A dolphin uses **echolocation** to get around. The dolphin makes clicks. The clicks echo in the sea. When the dolphin hears the echos, it can tell where things are.

Did you know?

A dolphin "hears" an echo with its jawbones.

Dolphin Families

Male dolphins are called **bulls**. Female dolphins are **cows**. A baby dolphin is a **calf**. A calf is born in the water. It drinks its mother's milk. It stays with its mother for up to eight years.

Did you know?

A newborn calf weighs about 40 pounds (18 kilograms).

Life in a Pod

Dolphins live in groups called **pods**. Most pods have about 30 dolphins. A pod works together to stay safe and to get food.

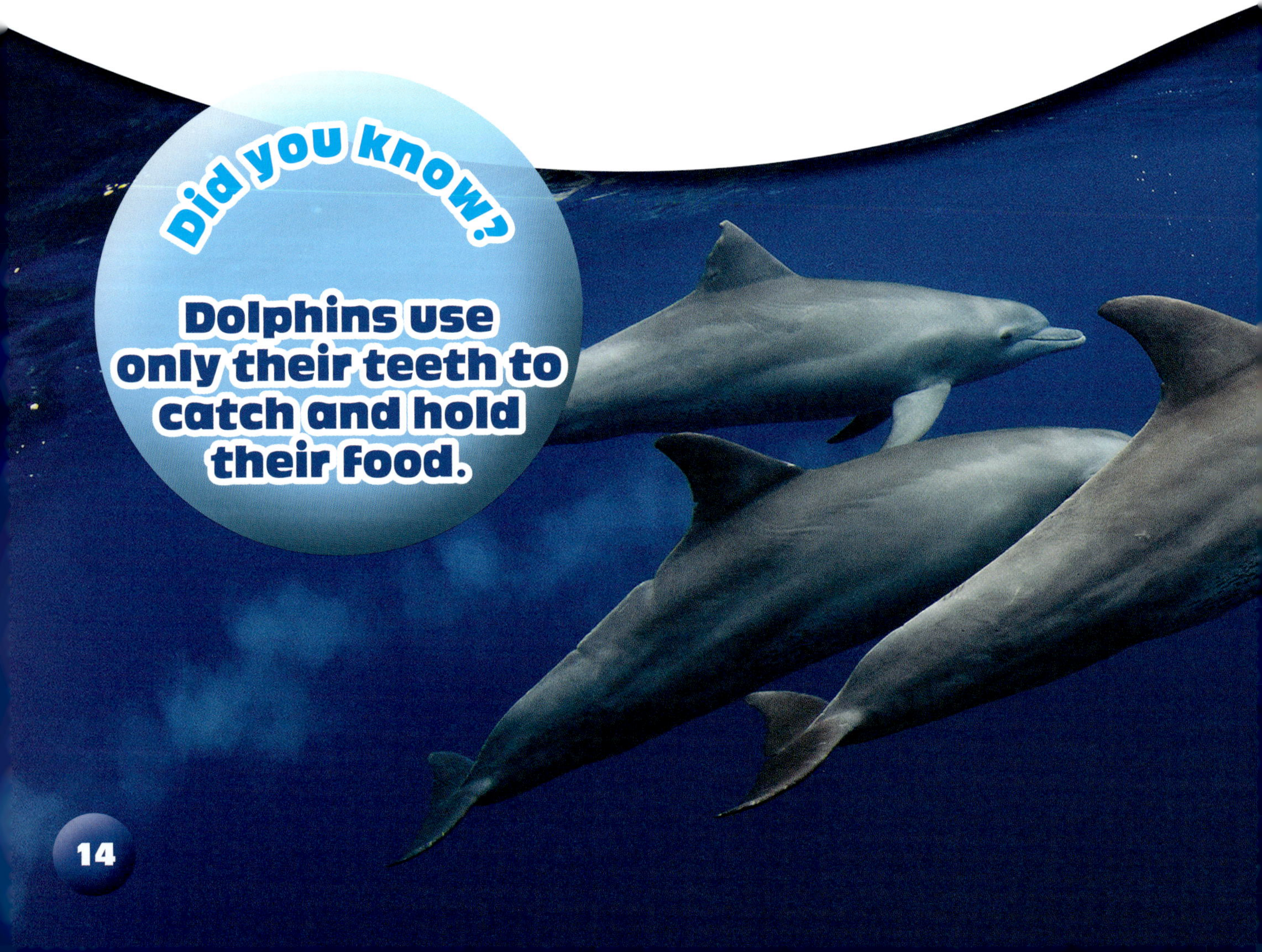

Did you know?

Dolphins use only their teeth to catch and hold their food.

Dolphins like to eat fish and squid. They do not chew their food. They swallow it in one piece.

Smart Dolphins

Dolphins are very smart. They use tools. They play. They "talk." They use sounds and splashes to say where they are. They can ask for help. They can give warnings.

Did you know?

Dolphins sometimes play with things such as sponges.

Dolphins can learn tricks. They can also learn to help people.

Some dolphins have been trained to find things in the water. Some have even saved people!

Dolphins are in danger. The sea is changing. They are losing places to live. People are working to help dolphins stay wild, healthy, and safe.

Did you know?

Dolphins live for about 20 to 40 years.

GLOSSARY

blowhole (BLOH-hohl): The hole on the top of a dolphin's head that it uses to breathe air is called a blowhole.

bull (BUL): A male dolphin is called a bull.

calf (KAFF): A baby dolphin is called a calf.

cow (KOW): A female dolphin is called a cow.

echolocation (ek-oh-loh-KAY-shun): A way of using echos to tell where things are is called echolocation. Dolphins use echolocation to find things in the dark sea.

flippers (FLIP-purz): Flippers are rounded limbs some animals have instead of arms and legs. Flippers help dolphins steer.

flukes (FLOOKS): Flukes are the two halves at the end of a dolphin's tail.

mammal (MAM-mull): A mammal is an animal that has warm blood. Mammal mothers feed their babies milk from their bodies. Dolphins and people are mammals.

pod (POD): A group of dolphins is called a pod.

species (SPEE-sheez): A type of a certain animal. There are more than 30 species of dolphins.

TO LEARN MORE

On the Web

Visit our Web page for lots of links about dolphins:
www.childsworld.com/links

Note to parents, teachers, and librarians: We routinely verify our Web links to make sure they are safe, active sites—so encourage your readers to check them out!

In the Library

Evans, Shira. *Dive, Dolphin!* Washington, DC: National Geographic Children's Books, 2016.

Kenan, Tessa. *Look, A Dolphin!* Minneapolis, MN: Lerner Publications, 2016.

Pfeffer, Wendy. *Dolphin Talk: Whistles, Clicks, and Clapping Jaws.* New York, NY: HarperCollins, 2003.

INDEX

About the Author

Kara L. Laughlin is an artist and writer who lives in Virginia with her husband, three kids, two guinea pigs, and a dog. She is the author of two dozen nonfiction books for kids.